Hope in the 2020s

HOPE

IN THE 2020s

ENCOURAGEMENT FOR OUR TIME

LAKE
DRIVE
lakedrivebooks.com

Lake Drive Books
6757 Cascade Road SE, 162
Grand Rapids, MI 49546

info@lakedrivebooks.com
lakedrivebooks.com
@lakedrivebooks

Publishing books that help you heal, grow, and discover.

Paperback ISBN: 978-1-957687-22-3
eBook ISBN: 978-1-957687-23-0

Cover photo by Eberhard Grossgasteiger on Pexels

Contents

Introduction

The 2020s got off to a rough start. January 21, 2020, marked the first known case of the virus that causes COVID-19, completely altering our society in the United States and causing millions of people to get sick and one million deaths as of this writing.

George Floyd was killed May 25, 2020, in an act of police brutality that re-ignited conflict over the ongoing racism and inequalities that so many want to pretend are not there.

A rancorous four-year political season culminated on January 6, 2021, in an angry mob of supporters of outgoing President Donald Trump that vandalized the U.S. Capitol building, threatened the safety of political leaders, and caused a number of deaths and countless cases of trauma.

On February 24, 2022, an authoritarian-led Russia invaded Ukraine seemingly because its leader felt threatened at the expansion of pro-democracy countries joining NATO. The relative global peace in the post-WWII era almost seems up for grabs. What's more, if the pandemic hadn't already created a challenge for our economy in stagnant wages, inflation, and supply chain issues, Russia's war in Ukraine put that challenge at a higher level.

The effects of climate change seem to be more obvious every year, with more summertime forest fires in the West and storms in the East, and that's just in the United States. Psychologists have acknowledged that climate anxiety is real.

School mass shootings, unconscionably, seem a regular occurrence, the suicide rate is up among teens, and there seems to be an ongoing loneliness epidemic. We're often split off from each other in our own news and social media enclaves. Even our churches, often thought to be the glue holding us together, have disappointed so many.

The scope of these problems cannot be underestimated, and they have no doubt heightened our stress levels. Solving today's challenges will take organizing and leadership in our local, national, and global communities. While there's much work to do, any efforts to bring light and improvement begin with the basic unit of hope that can and inevitably must be given voice on the individual level—units of hope especially in spite of hopelessness.

Hope springs eternal, as we like to say, but where do we find that spring? Let's take that analogy further. One of the things about natural springs is that, geologically speaking, underground water can build up pressure simply by the work of gravity, such as water inside a hill or a mountain. Sometimes you only need to pound a steel pipe into the ground at the bottom of that hill or mountain and the pressure will cause water to spout from the pipe, seemingly without end.

So too with us humans. We have hope always building up inside us, both individually and collectively. There's a gravitational pull to it, and it's hard to stop it no matter how cynical we sometimes become.

Hope in the 2020s is an attempt to tap into that refreshing water for the time we live in. Each of the essay contributors that follow offer an antidote, repellent, Patronus charm, or some method to catapult them into hope.

The 2020s don't seem to be getting any easier, that's for sure. We're perhaps living in a decade that will likely be seen as an historical turning point, but to what we're turning to is anybody's guess, and we're going to need to find hope wherever we can.

David Morris
Publisher
Lake Drive Books

You may not always have a comfortable life and you will not always be able to solve all of the world's problems at once but don't ever underestimate the importance you can have because history has shown us that courage can be contagious and hope can take on a life of its own.

Michelle Obama

Hope in Honesty and Loyalty

Lemuel R.T. Blackett

For some time, I have felt distant from friends that I have grown up with and some that I have recently met over the past ten years. Over the last few months, I have not felt any connection at all. About two months ago, a colleague of mine came out to San Diego to visit with me for a week. We played golf, had lunch, and just hung out.

As we got closer to the end of his trip, I started asking questions about different television shows he may like or new movies that have been released. To my surprise, of all the movies and shows that I liked, he had no interest. So, I jokingly asked, what do we have in common? He jokingly said "nothing." I chuckled and thought more deeply about his response. He's not into golf like I am, and though we are in the same profession we have two completely different philosophical ways of thinking of how it should be done. So why are we friends if there is no commonality, why do we use the word friend? With some of the friendships you have there is very little in common; however, you enjoy one another's vibe and personality. On the other side, you can have friends where you have so much in common, but you are not really friends, you just enjoy the same things.

The deeper reason behind my line of questioning comes from me witnessing other mutual friends disregard their commitment to friendship. One thing that bugs me about people is that they lack the ability to be honest. There is so much dishonesty in the world that you hope to find a safe space amongst family and friends.

Unfortunately, that is not the case in my situation. I recently found out that someone who I thought was loyal turned out to be an informant. Unbeknownst to me, they were feeding information to someone who used it to destroy an organization. After hearing this, I was taken aback, completely bewildered. I couldn't believe a mutual colleague would stoop so low, and that they did this just to gain a higher-ranking position. I've learned that some people will stop at nothing and hurt whoever they can just to get what they want. To be honest I lost hope in this person and the institution. I was already feeling on edge and distant and all this did was solidify my intuition.

I found it difficult to manage this new information. It opened old wounds that I thought I was over, and it put me in a place of seclusion. I no longer desired to be connected to this person in any way. My trauma was triggered, and my mental health was at stake. So, what did I do to get through this hurtful time? Several things come to mind.

1. I took a step back. That is a healthy thing to do. Sometimes taking a step back to examine yourself or re-

examine a situation will give you some clarity and closure. Taking a step back frees you from being engaged in a situation that will deplete you of your authentic self. Taking a step back shows you how to navigate through muddy waters.

2. I asked myself are these the type of people I want in my inner circle? Your inner circle is supposed to be filled with like-minded individuals that are pursuing the same goal; however, they may be exploring a multiplicity of options to reach that goal. If your inner circle is not fueling your vision or steering you in the right direction, then you may have to reevaluate your circle.

3. Investigate why being empathetic was affecting my emotions. Having empathetic characteristics is not a bad thing, however, if not used wisely it can consume you, and once you have been roped in, you can easily lose yourself while trying to help others find themselves.

4. Lastly, where do I find hope? I find hope in my time of quiet devotion. I find hope when I've done the best that I can, and I accept the results of my involvement whether good, bad, or indifferent. I find hope in believing in myself and my ability to rewrite the narrative. I find hope in the beauty that all things are possible when you believe.

Finding hope in times like these can be frustrating and taxing on the mind. So much transpires in our daily world and if we are overwhelmed by it, we must find some relief.

Find hope in knowing that you have some qualities to make this world better. Find hope in your children, realizing that you have the opportunity to instill into them some wisdom that can help them circumvent some unnecessary misfortunes. Find your hope in the Good Samaritan (like a true friend who is honest with you, despite your differences) that is not looking for a photo op but living to serve others without the pomp and circumstance. Find hope in every day where you are allowed to breathe because the whole day is not promised. Find hope in the smallest things that bring you the greatest joy.

Lemuel R.T. Blackett
lemuelblackett.org
Help, I'm Dealing with Trauma: Real Talk,
Real Encouragement, Real Healing

Since I was young, I have always known
this: Life damages us, every one. We
can't escape that damage. But now, I am
also learning this: We can be mended.
We mend each other.

Veronica Roth

Yes; &

Cynthia Vacca Davis

"I want to believe there's hope." I said to Jim, my therapist. The quest for hope was what led me to his office; it was all I wanted. One of my most important relationships had dissolved and life as I knew it unraveled. I was in the market for statistics, for truisms. I wanted Jim to say, "these situations always work out."

Instead, I got a primer on ambiguous grief—trauma that festers without closure. The losses that lead to this type of grief are, themselves, indefinite: the missing person who may or may not be found, the rift that might be permanent, but could also heal, the hope that justice will prevail, and the knowledge that it may not. Ambiguous loss is intangible—it's real, but it's also based on conjecture. An unconfirmed tragedy. Ambiguous grief forces us to hold two potential outcomes as equally true; to cling to one is to deny the truth of the other. You must carry gut-wrenching pain alongside the knowledge that relief may come in a week, a decade, or, just as likely, never.

Research tells us that people do better with finality than sustained, looming uncertainty. Author Oliver Burkeman noted in *The Guardian* that people who are widowed recover more fully—despite the greater initial pain—than people whose careers implode. There is a relief that finality gives us that allows us to heal. Hope tugs at us all the time: if this one thing changes everything will be fine.

No doubt because he knows all these truths, Jim had disappointingly little to offer regarding hope, beyond quoting a quasi-Buddhist maxim that "perhaps the greatest hope is to give up hope."

He may as well have told me to give up on life itself. Give up on my family being whole and healed? How could I ever do that?

The next appointment I made was with a tattoo parlor.

If you ask about my tattoo and I don't know you, I'll probably keep it light and say that the stylized "Yes; &" I had etched on my wrist has something to do with contradiction and opposition: yes, happiness and sadness, joy and pain, hate and love can be simultaneous emotions. Yes, one thing, and, also, the other. If I'm feeling philosophical, I might quote Rilke: "No feeling is final," or cite the "yes, and" thinking—comma, not semicolon—foundational to improv comedy and board room brainstorming. Yes, that thing, and this one, too; yes, what he said, and, also, what she said.

But the more vulnerable, more true, answer is that my tattoo is a scar. Something about my ambiguous pain had to be tangible. And I wanted to embrace the idea that my reality could expand to hold more than my hurt. That there was more to life.

And then, suddenly it seemed that the entire world was plummeted into a kind of collective of ambiguous grief. We found ourselves in the midst of a virus, a cultural reckoning, political upheaval, and economic chaos. My father, a newscaster by trade, told me that he has never seen the world so fragile, despite beginning his career in the late 1960s.

Fragile sounds scary.

We don't know the future of the virus—we can't predict if it will weaken or if we'll continue to be surprised by new variants. We can't predict if our vaccines will continue to work, or if the housing market will turn, or gas prices will stabilize. We don't have a handle on global warming. We're afraid the center won't hold.

But fragile things are also precious. I am coming to the place now where I view my "Yes; &" philosophy and "giving up on hope" as separate doors to the same life-giving place: the wild and wonderful present in all its marvelous and terrible complexity.

What this looks like is shifting my focus from an imaginary future that might never happen or could look radically different than anything I could predict in exchange for a eyes-wide-open look at the here and now.

Yes, the news hurts my heart and, also, my husband just made me the most delicious salad and served it with crisp, fruity wine on our shady patio.

Yes, the relationship I miss is still broken, and I also have a wider social circle than I have ever had before.

Yes, there's an ache of loss and there's also gut-splitting laughter and family and chosen family.

Yes, there's uncertainty and there's possibility.

And perhaps possibility, laced with gratitude, is the closest to hope that I have ever been.

Cynthia Vacca Davis
cynthiavaccadavis.com
Intersexion: A Story of Faith, Identity, and Authenticity

So don't be frightened, dear friend, if a sadness confronts you larger than any you have ever known, casting its shadow over all you do. You must think that something is happening within you, and remember that life has not forgotten you; it holds you in its hand and will not let you fall. Why would you want to exclude from your life any uneasiness, any pain, any depression, since you don't know what work they are accomplishing within you?

Rainer Maria Rilke

Embers of Hope Dance from the Fires of Trauma

Rebekah Drumsta

When you're a trauma survivor, hope can be hard.

With every fiber of your being you want to be a hopeful person, but considering your history, the times people have harmed, betrayed, abused, or let you down can just add up to a feeling of caution, anxiety, hypervigilance, or apathy. Hope isn't something you can fake. Toxic positivity, now that's a thing you can make up or engage as a masking behavior while you mirror others around you.

I say, look for the sparkles.

Have you ever been dehydrated and started seeing spots in your eyes? Or maybe stared into the sun and regretted it seconds later? Even better yet, have you enjoyed a gooey s'more around a campfire while watching little embers float toward the sky? That's what I mean by sparkles. Little glimmers of something that wasn't there before which intrigues or piques your curiosity. Sometimes distracting, sometimes there to help us recognize a need or just take the time to refocus.

My own lived experience has led me to learn more specifically about religious trauma. Classically, religious environments do not prioritize mental health, often expressing criticism or skepticism, and have, in fact, created a space where individuals must disassociate from their emotions in order to follow spiritual expectations. No sparkles gleaming there.

In the first-ever quantitative sociological study on religious trauma, the Global Center for Religious Research found that eleven percent of survey respondents said they have never suffered from religious trauma despite also claiming that they currently suffer from three of the six major trauma symptoms.[1] In other words, while still in the minority, people were either uninformed or unwilling to acknowledge their history with religious trauma. This, to me, is a sign that more work needs to be done in raising awareness, but it also brings to question why people with religious backgrounds often lack keenness of emotional understanding.

Since the beginning of the 2020s, my own life has been impacted by friends who have lost children unexpectedly, job loss and housing transition, separation from family and friends, the tension of a world in turmoil and seemingly on fire, relationships changing around me, and Christianity in America acting out like an entitled, spoiled human.

---

[1] https://www.gcrr.org/religioustrauma

Thanks to lockdowns, forced alterations of routine and people having some time to think and process, the church has been conducted into a compulsory wakeup call. Waves of people have begun to recognize the spiritual abuse or unhealthy control they were living under, which opened doors for faith deconstruction (or disentangling, if that word has a more palatable vibe for you) and increased religious trauma recognition.

I have observed that with this cultural shift and collective awakening comes a reclaiming of one's own spiritual autonomy: meaning individuals are seeking God and working out their faith in accordance with their own conscience, research, and experience instead of relying on the theologies and doctrines handed down by denominations, spiritual leaders, family, and tradition. The Bible and Christian faith have once again been placed into the hands of the people and removed from the shackles of "the chosen few" who alone can interpret and speak on behalf of God. And this is one of my hope sparkles. The more we understand how toxic and authoritarian religion harms people, the more we can help those who are hurting and help stop it from happening.

Last year my family loaded into our RV and drove from Texas to spend some time camping in New Mexico. Wild horses frequently meandered through our campground. Watching a free-range foal explore and dart around was a highlight of that adventure. Forest fires were active that season with many still burning, causing smoke to drift our way from time to time. During that trip, we made a stop at Smokey Bear National Park where we learned the true story of the real Smokey Bear. It was in the middle of an educational video that I had a moment which changed my perspective on the church today. The film explained that when the situation is right, forest fires can be started with merely a spark. This can devastate and destroy thousands of acres at a time, devouring everything in its path, leaving behind only ashes and charred remnants. As the blaze sweeps, it removes oxygen from the air with metal-melting temperatures. Then time passes. Rains come, animals start to return, and nature begins the process of regeneration. Often after intense fires, as the foliage appears again, certain varieties of plants appear that previously had been rare or thought gone from that area's ecosystem. Life that had been buried or hidden resurfaces.

Sitting in that tiny national park theatre it dawned on me: this my hope for Christianity in America. The dead, the unhealthy, the thick underbrush, the sickness that has endangered or consumed the church and western faith— that is what is being burned today. It feels like destruction. It feels like chaos. People are feeling the heat, some struggling to breathe. A burning is happening in people's hearts. Embers swim overhead, as what we have always known is altered. When the smoke clears, it looks like the Church, like Christianity could be gone forever. And honestly, that pile over there smoldering, that part needed burning to the ground because—oh because—beneath the ashes is the life that had survived underground. A burn sometimes is necessary to bring back life, add protection, and maintain health.

The world doesn't need more million follower influencers. The world doesn't need more Christians who write books, preach sermons, lead seminars, and build ministries with their name on it. The world needs more real humans doing human things such as saying out loud, "I am recovering from trauma and finding hope is hard." The world needs more real humans who say, "American Christianity has to change, and it starts with me."

I'm watching grassroots action all around me. There's no single leader in the deconstruction movement. It's people like you and me who've said, "I was hurt. I want to help people. I want to be the change." Rarely does true reformation start at the top: first, it begins as a warm glow in the hearts of ordinary people then finally becomes such a roaring blaze that those in power must pay heed and humbly change or become obsolete. Fundamentalism and evangelicalism have become kindling for a holy inferno that is fueled by strength, truth, and justice.

So, for the rest of this decade, as you journey through religious trauma, through shifts and shakings of your faith, through the challenges and changes of the 2020s, remember: hope sparkles up and over the crackling heat. Know that good will come again. Those sparkling embers may disappear, but they existed. You did see the light, if ever so briefly. Out of the fire dance embers of hope.

Rebekah Drumsta
rebekahdrumsta.com
When Family Hurts: 30 Days to
Finding Healing and Clarity

"Me and you, we got more yesterday than anybody. We need some kind of tomorrow."

Toni Morrison, *Beloved*

Hope in a Bigger God

Trey Ferguson

We make God sound so small sometimes. Petty. Fragile.

Entire systematic theologies articulating exactly who (or what) God is have been constructed, disseminated, and passed down for centuries now. We got the cute lil' acronyms and everything (looking at you, TULIP). I'll be real with you—that kinda god don't sound too good to me. The love of this god even seems sorta like hate from time to time. This god ain't worried about faith. Certainty is rewarded in his kingdom. Hope is folly in the world ruled by this tiny god. What good is hope when we are already certain about the course this god would take us on?

This god has condemned our imagination. Our imagination has been cast into the lake of fire, where there is weeping and gnashing of teeth. Without imagination, there is no hope. There is just the tomorrow we cannot muster up the energy to look forward to. We dread the future this teeny god has authored for us.

Or maybe it's just me. I could be projecting.

It's weird. Technology has done a number on what we are able to envision for ourselves. The smart phone reshaped the western world in the past fifteen years. Twitter gave us access to news headlines faster than ever before. It was dope. At first. But then the news got sort of... well... depressing. On top of that, social media also gave us access to everyone's thoughts. And if we're being honest? A lot of those thoughts stink. Ain't it funny? The same technology that placed entire libraries into the palms of our hands also made everybody's family reunions super uncomfortable. We gotta decide if we're gonna pretend we didn't see Uncle Jimbo go full Archie Bunker on Facebook, or if we're gonna give him a piece of our mind.

The Jetsons had us ready for flying cars by now. The cutting edge of technology left us with people wanting to "Make America Great Again" instead.

Indeed, our imagination is shot.

But what if God is really a creator? And what if humans are really created in the image of God? Not the small, petty, fragile god—but the God whose Spirit hovered over the chaos before the beginning began to begin? What if we can find hope in a bigger God? What if this God not only is desperately committed to saving our souls, but also redeeming our imaginations as well? That would require faith in something we have yet to see. That sounds like the type of stuff I'm into.

I get the appeal of asceticism. Monks are onto something. The fact of the matter is I'm too far down the other road by now. A wife and some kids—I can't just pack up and choose a monastery at this point. So I gotta grind it out here. The idea that we can just leave behind everything we know and live a whole different life, though? That's dope. That takes courage. Chasing wholeness over familiarity sounds good until you're faced with the decision yourself. And since many of us cannot choose the monastic life, we must choose another way.

We must choose to live in hope.

The small, petty, fragile god who has arrested, caged, and condemned our imagination is pleased when we stay stuck. His right worship is the status quo. Progress is heresy. Renewal is rejection. Hope is a slippery slope.

If God is a creator, and that Creator made humanity in God's own image, then this other god is a pretender. And so we must abandon that false god. We must tear down his high places and his altars. We must shame his priests.

James Baldwin once prophetically declared, "If the concept of God has any validity or any use, it can only be to make us larger, freer, and more loving. If God cannot do this, then it is time we got rid of Him." Because the God of creation never stops creating. Yes, rest is divine. But so is drawing people out of bondage into the wilderness where new identities and conventions are forged among them.

The hope that shapes tomorrow is tied to a bigger God than the one this nation was built under. This gigantic God has been there the whole time, calling for us just beyond the cages the tiny god has constructed around us. This bigger God has freed our imagination from its cell, begging us to come and join them on the other side of our hopelessness. This God offers us hope as liturgy. Progress is not contraband in the reign of this God. Joy and rest are the currencies that matter. They appear whenever true worship—love and justice—have been carried out.

Like a midwife, hope stands ready to deliver us into the waiting arms of a God who is far bigger than we've been able to conceptualize while separated from our imaginations. The God who created—before the beginning began to begin—is present. Holding the hand of our imagination. Ready for a reunion. Ready to inspire. Ready to rehumanize. There is no limit to where hope can lead you, for the God who authored it exists beyond the scope of every thought we've ever had.

There is hope in a bigger God still.

Trey Ferguson
pastortrey05.com
host of the *New Living Treyslation*
and co-host of *Three Black Men*

Listen to the mustn'ts, child. Listen to
the don'ts. Listen to the shouldn'ts, the
impossibles, the won'ts. Listen to the
never haves, then listen close to me...
Anything can happen, child.
Anything can be.

Shel Silverstein

Hope Is Not a Feeling—It's Fuel

Brandon Darrell Lane Flanery

Hope is not a feeling—it's fuel.

Let me explain...

Once upon a time, I dated a guy who liked to climb mountains.

Problem: I didn't like to climb mountains. And neither did my friends. But magically, upon meeting this man, I, mysteriously, began to like climbing mountains (funny how that works).

Then he made us climb one...

With heavy packs and terrible shoes, four of us lugged up an alpine pass, back down into a valley, and up again to the other side. The mountains we were hiking were called the Sangre de Christo: the blood of Christ, and they would be our penance. For what you may ask? I have no fucking clue. But it must have been bad, really bad.

Like five-year-old children, my friends and I kept asking the boy who liked mountains, "Are we there yet?"

"Just another five minutes," he'd reply.

Our ankles were swollen, and our backs were bent, but we'd continue. Hope had become our fuel. We were almost there! We could do this! Just take another step!

...till another five minutes ...and another five minutes ... and another ...for two miserable hours.

"What the hell is going on? Have you been lying to us the whole time?"

"Almost! Just another five minutes. I promise I'm not lying this time. It'll be worth it."

"Why should we believe you?"

While hope is fuel, hope deferred is a brick wall.

You start the engine. Hit the accelerator. Build up speed. Thinking a magical journey up a magical mountain awaits you. But instead of magic, you've crashed into a black and yellow bullseye like the dummy you are, broken bones and bleeding heart.

While I don't have any broken bones, my heart has bled plenty of times, and I'm not just talking about a shitty mountain trip.

After coming out of evangelicalism and the closet, I've become somewhat of a cynic. The former made me question all the good and the latter made me brace for all the bad, and all for good reasons...

...Realizing that so much of what I believed has hurt people.

...Beginning to doubt what is true after so many lies.

...Losing a career in ministry after giving so much time and money.

...Betrayed by friends and family who always talked about unconditional love.

After all of it, I ultimately believe my cynicism keeps me safe, a shelter from the storm, while hope is for schmucks caught in a gale.

After an eight-hour hike, storm clouds rolled in, and the sun began to set.

"We need to stop for camp," we said. "We can continue tomorrow."

"Five more minutes."

We pushed through the rain and continued on in the dark. We had come so far. We couldn't give up now. At some point late into the night, we made it to our destination.

The boy who liked to climb mountains began to try and start a fire so we could cook our food. We were starving and cold. Hot beans sounded so nice.

While my friends pitched the tent, I gave the boy whatever dry moss and sticks I could find for kindling.

Eventually, we made a fire and gathered around to keep warm.

No one spoke. We just ate and crawled into bed. The boy and I had to share a sleeping bag because the other one got wet.

My friends and I had no idea what we were doing or what we were getting ourselves into. All we knew was that we were mad. Really mad.

Then morning came...

As the sun crept over the mountains, its rays warmed us awake. The boy who likes mountains shook me up, and he grabbed his fishing pole.

As I hemmed and hawed, stretching my back and wiping away crust from my eyes, I took in the scene...

...A turquoise alpine lake.

...A singing brook weaving through the trees.

...A tall granite cliff.

...A sprawling colorful valley.

...Greens and grays.

...Blue skies above.

...Yellow wildflowers below.

I sucked in the crisp mountain air.

"I told you it would be worth it," the boy who likes mountains said.

And in that moment, I liked them too.

Hope is fuel; it got us up the mountain.

And cynicism is shelter; it hides me from the storm.

But something is wiggling inside me lately: If I never hope, I still lose.

Sure, those who hope may be conned, but at least for a moment they're happy.

Sure, those who trust may get robbed, but at least at one point they had possessions.

Sure, we may get suckered up the mountain, but at least we saw an alpine lake.

While hope deferred and betrayal suck, shaking our foundation, at least we had an up before we had a down.

I guess what I'm saying is, I'm starting to learn we all get hurt, regardless of if we hide in the house or climb the Blood of Christ. But wouldn't it be nice to hope for at least a little? Wouldn't it be nice to get excited about what's beyond the bend?

Which makes me realize hope is not just fuel, it's also an act, a courageous, idiotic act: a choice ...a lie even ...a performance, a performance that makes us smile, makes us laugh, makes us cry, makes us feel.

At the end of the day, I think feeling—both the good and the bad—is better than lying down before we ever rise.

And who knows, maybe this time, we'll actually rise.

Which brings me to my final point.

Yes, hope is fuel; yes, hope is an act; but most of all, I am learning that hope is doubt, doubt that maybe this time it won't go so wrong; that maybe this time it might not be so bad. Maybe, just maybe, this time our destination is around the next bend.

"Just five more minutes."

Brandon Darrell Lane Flanery
brandonflanery.com
Stumbling: A Sassy Memoir about
Coming Out of Evangelicalism

The very least you can do in your life is figure out what you hope for. And the most you can do is live inside that hope. Not admire it from a distance but live right in it, under its roof.

Barbara Kingsolver

Hope in What We are For

Matt Kendziera

Every generation has a handful of moments when everyone can remember where they were. For my generation, this includes the collapse of the twin towers of The World Trade Center on 9/11. For my parents it includes the assassination of JFK and MLK, and for my grandparents it was the bombing of Pearl Harbor. Inside these big events we all remember there are other events more specific to who we are. For me, one of those events was the tragic shooting at Columbine High School, when two boys entered a school with semiautomatic weapons and homemade bombs and opened fire, killing twelve students, one teacher, and themselves.

Nearly two decades after this tragic event, I found myself looking for new spaces to use my public speaking abilities as the evangelical Christian circles became something I could no longer do while still being able to look at myself in the mirror. I hopped on the computer and went to Indeed.com. In the search engine I typed in "motivational speaker." When it asked where I wanted to work, I simply typed, "United States." There was a single match that came up and it was for an organization out of Littleton, Colorado called Rachel's Challenge, an organization started by the father of one of the Columbine victims.

After her death, Rachel Scott's father, Darrell, committed his life to continuing the chain reaction of kindness and compassion that his daughter started when she was alive. He didn't take up a crusade against gun violence or bullying; instead, he used Rachel's life and story to inspire students and adults all over the world to simply care for one another. Darrell Scott made one decision that has changed the lives of millions of people throughout the world. He made a decision that I am not sure I would be capable of if I were in his shoes. He decided to be for something instead of against something. Like Darrell, Jesus didn't speak much about what he was against, but he did speak a great deal about what he was for.

Religion has become good at being against things and people when all Jesus desired was togetherness. The word he used during the only documented time he prayed was *unity* (John 17). That we would be for each other and with each other in the same way he and his father are for each other and with each other. Instead, the church has often preached a message of division. If you are on the inside and you serve, give, and believe correctly, you will receive all the benefits it has to give. But as soon as you don't fit or you question the foundation on which it is built, you are no longer allowed to be a beneficiary. Even in our time, several prominent authors who have written and spoken messages that go against the grain have been publicly excommunicated from the church after being their poster children for years.

True community should not be defined by having the same beliefs, but by having similar hearts. What many of us experienced was, for the most part, a cheap substitution for something that is real and beautiful. It's like saying sex with a prostitute is true intimacy. It's not. The moment you stop paying it goes away. In the same way, many church gatherings do not represent true community. Because when you leave, you lose. I don't think I have met a single person who has left the church without losing most of their friends.

Many of you reading this have gone through very difficult situations regarding church and faith. The reason you are looking for a change is that you have found enough wrong with what you were a part of. It is important to find time and space to talk through the hurts and disappointments you experienced. It is equally important to stop focusing on them at some point so you can move forward in a healthy and meaningful way. Believe me when I say that this is much easier said than done, and we must be careful not to rush the process. Some are able to move forward quickly, with an almost supernatural ability to forgive and see with new perspective. For others like myself, it was and, in some ways, still is a long and grueling journey, filled with a lot of anger, frustration, hurt, and disappointment. Through my healing process, one lesson I have learned is that the longer we hold onto the hurt and disappointment, the longer it holds onto us.

What is important is not so much what we are running away from, but what we are walking toward.

After I presented for Rachels' Challenge at an event in Pennsylvania, a young woman approached me with a journal in her hands. She thanked me for being there and flipped to the front of her journal. She looked me in the eyes and said, "In the front on this journal are all of the reasons I didn't believe I should be on this earth; all of the reasons that I was going to kill myself." She then flipped to the back of the journal and continued. "After hearing Rachel's story, I decided I want to live, and these are all of the reasons I belong here and all of the reasons I need to be alive." That is what is possible when we are brave enough to worry less about what we are against and decide what it is we are for.

Matt Kendziera
mattkendziera.com
Bring It Home: The Adventure of Finding Yourself after Being Lost in Religion

Many things are possible for the person who has hope. Even more is possible for the person who has faith. And still more is possible for the person who knows how to love. But everything is possible for the person who practices all three virtues.

Brother Lawrence

Finding Hope in the Small Things

Kate J. Meyer

I write and speak about hope a lot. Not for any particular reason, really; just because I know that, for me at least, hope can sometimes be the only thing to carry a person through the day. It is far too easy to give up and turn inward when things are dark, when things (homes? hearts? lives?) are breaking, when nothing is going as planned, when a way out seems impossible to find. To me, hope is the thing that prevents the inward turn and sustains a person to keep going. I can't define it, but I know what it is. I can't pinpoint it, but I know it when I feel it.

I've experienced several seasons of life during which I intensely sought hope because it was clear to me that hope was the only way I was going to be able to endure. Such seasons can be limited to a facet of my life or impact my life as a whole; the source doesn't much matter. What matters is honing one's skills to seek hope, rather than waiting for hope to find you.

When I was asked to share where I find hope in a time of a pandemic, war, high gas costs, racism-imploding, hatred-dense season of life, I took a lot of time to ponder how to name it, how to put it into words that both resonate and successfully translate. And then it hit me. I find hope in the seemingly small moments that interrupt the anxiety and lift the gloom, even if for but a moment.

In just one week, these are pockets of hope I either witnessed or participated in:

...a grieving widow who experienced her first belly laugh since her spouse's death,

...a lunch that was filled with laughter and genuine connection with a friend I hadn't seen in over a year,

...listening to a friend begin a conversation with self-deprecating comments, and end the conversation knowing those comments were false, and then her being able to speak her truth,

...an unexpected phone call with my best friend, both serious and silly,

...learning story after story of people being freed from religious shame,

...seeing grass grow, birds return, and feeling a cool breeze after early season sticky Midwest humidity,

...driving to a work visit dreading the need to fill my gas tank and finding a station along the way that is thirteen cents cheaper than anywhere else,

...a pharmacy rep working with a savings card rep via three-way call with me to erase an insurmountable pharmacy co-pay,

...seeing a growing legion of Jesus followers rise up and name the atrocities to which the Church has been, at minimum, complicit, and knowing these same followers are the soon-to-be leaders of the Church,

...being the first woman in a pulpit in a church less than an hour from my home,

...stopping my lawn mower to take a call from an inner circle friend who wanted to share her own resurgence of hope.

You see, hope is not one consistent current running through life. Hope is found in what some would call the small moments of life, that are, in that moment, a big thing in the world of the person experiencing it. Hope is a shift in perspective, the ability to pause and wonder and dream, the ability to rest and laugh even if only for a moment.

I think the changing nature of hope is what makes it so difficult to define and to share. But that changing nature is also what I most love about hope. If hope was something we could conjure at will, I'm afraid it would lose its power. We'd become immune to its effects and, let's be honest, we need the jolt hope provides. Especially in today's world.

The key is to keep eyes, ears, and hearts open to catch hope when it presents itself. Hope is meant to be the cushion on which to land when things are falling apart, the thing that tells us that though we can't see it or understand it, somehow there is a reason to keep going. When we're in the muck of it, though, it is easy to miss the moment the cushion makes its appearance, especially since it usually occurs only briefly. The current state of the country (and the world) can leave us living on high alert, anxious, ready to debate and defend, and to be suspicious of, well, everything. And that stance is what results in hope flying by uncaught. Why? Because keeping to that level of alertness means there is no capacity for the body or the brain to relax and exist in the present, and the present is where hope happens. Hope is here and now.

When I am at my most defeated, regardless of the cause of the current defeat, I have learned the first move I need to make is to get my brain out of the future and into the present. In the present I can hear what people are saying, instead of planning my retort. In the present I can recognize that right now, in this moment, all is well; and why would I want to steal that from myself? In the present, I can hear nature around me and live for a moment in the awe and wonder of creation. Those are the places hope thrives and the moments the cushion of hope is floated to us. Hope doesn't change the reality or take away the pain, but hope does empower us to continue, to feel lighter, and to see with greater clarity.

Hope. I might not always catch it, but when I do, I find it in what you might see as something small; but from my vantage point, it's everything.

Kate J. Meyer, LPC, MDiv
katejmeyer.com
Faith Doesn't Erase Grief: Embracing the
Experience and Finding Hope

The very existence of libraries affords
the best evidence that we may yet have
hope for the future of man.

T.S. Eliot

Reading Brings Hope

David Morris

The 2020s have been a time when it's way too easy to be thought-less and insensitive. We turn a blind eye to the realities right in front of us, along with the opportunities to do better. We rush into condemnation before taking the time to understand what we are condemning. We sift the world through a strainer where everything and everyone becomes something to hold back or let through.

I've caught myself doing it, and who hasn't?

We humans can be uncooperative: so much heresy hunting, false equivalencies, obfuscation, manufactured controversies, and outright hatred. I sometimes get so angry at so much of this callousness that my wife looks at me while we're on a neighborhood walk with our sweet little dog and asks, "Are you ok?"

During the pandemic, book sales and reading were on a rise. In other words, when the world seems like it's crumbling, books often become a saving grace, and the uptick in my pandemic reading habit has lingered and it has been a help, a balm, and a source of imagination.

I find hope in reading. I learn, and better piece things together. I get a better sense of perspective. I grow.

No one can touch what happens when you read good books. Here are some examples.

First, Daniel White Hodge's *Baptized in Dirty Water: Reimagining the Gospel according to Tupac Amaru Shakur* is about the spiritual message in Hip Hop culture, and specifically in the music, lyrics, actions, and events in the short life of Tupac Shakur.

Hodge starts by describing "soul" and "post-soul" culture. The former describes the 1960s Civil Rights movement when Black culture had clarity about right and wrong, much structured by Black churches and Black leaders like Martin Luther King Jr. The latter describes the time afterward where people of African descent still were failed by our social structures. The dividing line in racism continued, and people, including Christians, forgot about the often violent ghetto depicted in *Boyz in the Hood*. Hip Hop, Hodge explains, characterizes this post-soul era with its attempt to describe continued repressed anger, the lack of any new advocate, and to establish its own lifestyle and community.

With his growing up as the son of a mother who was a Black Panther leader, and with his interest in songwriting, the imperfect Tupac shaped a body of work that today still speaks to the Black experience with songs like "So Many Tears," about the God who seems to have given up on the ghetto, and Tupac's song writing about THUG LIFE (The Hate You Give Little Infants Fucks Everyone).

Reading Hodge's book, you can't help but open your favorite streaming app and start listening to this rhythmic, powerful, and explicit music. You can't help but notice the enigmatic and discordant chords, the lament in the vocals, and the mythological imagery in the lyrics. When I read this book and listen to this music, as a White guy, it helps me understand. I feel as though I'm looking through a portal to a world I had no idea existed. I feel ashamed that I'm part of the problem, as we all are part of the problem when people continue to suffer inequality, shame, and violence. It hurts to understand better, but it compels me to soften, and to learn more.

Second, I like to read Bart Ehrman books, or even better, to listen to his audio books and hear this former evangelical turned non-Christian bring light and understanding with the power and passion of an outspoken preacher. It's ironic.

Bart Ehrman is an American New Testament scholar who focuses on textual studies of the Bible, the historical Jesus, and the origins and development of early Christianity. He is also considered a public scholar, translating the detailed information he's uncovered into books that just about anyone can read and digest. They may be meticulous and at times complicated to read, but the takeaway is that the scripture you call holy and sacred has far more nuance and context than you might realize. It's fascinating, it's refreshing, and you'll wonder why your pastor never talked about these contexts in church.

Some of the letters of Paul were forged by other people? There really are outright inconsistencies in the Bible, some of which are emphasized and others ignored? Of all the holy texts circulating so many centuries ago, why are some in the Bible and not others, and who got to make the decisions about that?

Reading Ehrman can be dizzying, but every time I do, I feel like I'm on a vacation from so much cultural baggage that I've internalized all these years. It's a fun vacation, quite relaxing and perspective giving.

Third and finally, I recently discovered Anna Maria Rizzuto's *Why Did Freud Reject God? A Psychodynamic Interpretation?* So many religious people love to dismiss the famous Austrian psychoanalyst Sigmund Freud. With his emphasis on sexually charged psychological drives, some even say (quite hatefully), that he was the world's greatest pervert.

Having earned a doctorate in psychology and religion, I understand that Freud irritated religious people, but it's primarily because he developed a language to describe the inner life that used to be the primary domain of religion.

What's more, Freud was an iconoclast. He popularized the idea that we have thoughts, memories, and motivations that are not readily available to our everyday consciousness, yet they still shape our perceptions and behaviors. He saw psychoanalysis as a method to help make the unconscious conscious. That method generally makes people uncomfortable, including religious people who are unaware that some of the ways in which they participate in religion are often to meet self-serving needs.

Freud is also famous for hating religion, or so it seems. But what most people don't realize is that he couldn't stop writing about religion. He authored a good handful of short books on religion, much of it published in his later life. He also loved to collect mythological figurines with which he decorated his office.

Psychoanalyst Anna Maria Rizzuto picked up on the fact that Freud protests too much about religion. In her book, you learn that Freud enthusiastically attended a Catholic church as a toddler, and that he was intimately acquainted with the Hebrew Bible. One on hand, you learn these details and more, but on the other, and more importantly, you learn how the life events of Freud's upbringing contributed significantly to Freud's musings about religion.

Why Did Freud Reject God? actually proves Freud's own point. Our religious life is extraordinarily determined, and if we can uncover how, we might just learn something real about what's real.

There's something that happens when we deepen our understanding of the world around us by reading books that interest and fascinate us. When we understand better, it's one of the best kinds of hope there is. It's amazing actually.

David Morris

davidrmorris.me

Lost Faith and Wandering Souls: A Psychology of Disillusionment, Mourning, and the Return of Hope

Everyone must dream. We dream to give ourselves hope. To stop dreaming—well, that's like saying you can never change your fate. Isn't that true?

Amy Tan

The Pessimist's Dilemma

R. Scott Okamoto

I'm often accused of being cynical or pessimistic, probably because I'm very good at pointing out, in exquisite detail and with no small amount of irony, the shitty nature of life and human nature. And despite my humorous take, people often write me off as just a negative person. I've noticed over my life that non-Asian people tend to expect me to behave in a docile, tranquil manner, so when someone like me gets all up in his feelings about the world, well, hell hath no fury like an assumption shattered in a dull mind.

In my blog, I've pointed out problems in parenting and parent culture, evangelical Christianity, and sexual identities and relationships from a cis-het point of view. If you know anything about these things, you'd be correct in assuming I never lack for something to write about. I could spend a writer's-block-free lifetime dipping my pen into the infinite well of human brokenness, and I probably will. But I have to confess something: I may expect the worst, but I really do hope for the best.

I generally don't like parents, even though I am one. I mean, I like people, but when people come at me with parenting vibes, I tend to run away. What are parenting vibes? Acknowledging that there are wonderful exceptions to this horrible observation, take all the fear in the universe, mix it with a good dose of narcissism, a pinch of not-so-subtle competitiveness, and finish it off with six gallons of projection—that's a parenting vibe.

Parents act like everything bad in the universe can and will happen to their kids. At the same time, they, by the sheer force of their genetic makeup, have given birth to the next Picasso, Mozart, Shakespeare, Jonas Salk, or Jonas Brother. I guess this warrants their fears of harm to their precious progeny since so much is at stake for the world, should something happen to their child or children. Said parents will let you know about it all, too. And of course, anything the parent fears, enjoys, or hates is projected onto the children, and here I must admit guilt. Instead of railing against selfish, capitalistic, competitive parenting, I'll go after myself.

For example, I assumed my kids would like the same things I do, and I am 0 for 3. Three kids who hate sports, don't like playing guitar, and don't like fly fishing. I guess that's 0 for 9. My daughter has lately taken to fly fishing but for a while there I was batting .000 with my favorite things being passed down to my children.

And yet, my kids ...my fucking kids ...give me hope. The love they have for each other, for my wife and me, and for our community is so much bigger and life-giving than celebrating the 2020 Dodgers winning the World Series, shredding a sick guitar solo, or casting a dry fly to rising trout. Wait. I just re-read that last sentence, and now I'm not so sure because those things are awesome. I'm pretty sure the love is bigger and better than some of my favorite things. I hope it is anyway. Yeah ...yeah. It totally ...is.

Evangelicals. There are so many ...um ...there are a few ...uh ...that might be okay ...fuck. Nope. I have no hope here. Moving on. See my blog for more fun at evangelicals' expense. The only hope comes from the fact that so many are leaving, but even then, this deconstruction pipeline does not always filter out the racism, sexism, homophobia, transphobia, or false assumptions about the world so entrenched in evangelical culture. It's a start to get out, but it can be a long, difficult road to fuller humanity. This is why I came back from my amazing life away from anything to do with Christianity. I want to help people find their way out and into communities that promote love, equity, and inclusion. For now, evangelicals are the enemy of all those things.

Sex and sexuality. Hell yeah. From learning about and forming relationships with LGBTQIA communities to shedding the harmful, guilt-ridden purity culture bullshit of our past, the ex-evangelical/deconstruction movement is finding new ways of thinking about identity. Our sense of gender and sexuality were two of the most policed identities in evangelical culture, so it makes perfect sense that they become fertile ground for exploration. It's a long road that usually begins with forgiving oneself for any sexual "sin" committed pre-marriage, if someone is or was married, or freedom to explore one's sexuality if single.

One might even be able to explore sexuality as a married person if the partner gives consent. All this because, outside of evangelicalism, sex and sexuality are not clear in the Bible. Lots of wiggle room there with some awesome kink in the Old Testament. If a person deconstructs completely, a life lived outside of any biblical interpretations can be whatever a person desires, and there are many desires to explore, if a person so chooses.

The thing is, life has so much to offer, and I'm checking it all out. So, while I have the privilege to do so despite all the fucked-up shit in this world, I will. I will love fiercely. I will fight for your humanity, even if you don't recognize mine. And I will be fueled by hope that this life, fully and purposefully lived, will make a positive impact on this world. This hope comes from the love my kids share with each other and the world, from watching the demise of the evangelical Church, and from the idea that people are loving without fundamentalist, puritanical boundaries while discovering their identities through relationships and sexuality. It all even gives me hope that someday my kids will take me to a Dodgers game. It's never going to happen, and I've accepted that. But goddamn, what a dream to hope for. Who's the cynical pessimist now? Well, I guess it depends on the day, but generally, not me.

R. Scott Okamoto
rscottokamoto.com
Asian American Apostate: Losing Religion and Finding Myself at an Evangelical University

Hope is the thing with feathers that
perches in the soul and sings the tune
without the words and never stops at all.

Emily Dickinson

And When That Mockingbird Does Sing

Julia Rocchi

Good Friday service, 2022. My church's casement windows were thrown open to the warming spring day, almost too pretty for a solemn start to the Triduum. The air wafting in smelled green. The pews were not packed; everyone checkerboarded at safe distances and kept their masks tight against their cheeks. Outside, a mockingbird trilled, and when I opened my mouth to join the song, my own mask chafed.

Much of my formative church experience is marked by singing, both as an eager congregant and as a choir member from high school through college to my adult parishes. In fact, I met my husband through music ministry. We sang our favorite hymns to our older son as bedtime lullabies. But these days I rarely sing. I have one excuse after another—my allergies are flaring, we aren't physically at church, masks are claustrophobic—but the truth is, I just don't feel like it. When my younger son, still an infant, is ready for bed, I simply rock and pat him. No song or hum or chant. Only silence and my own thoughts, which often turn to sadness and despair over the current state of the world.

But on this Good Friday—two years into a global pandemic, and my first time back inside the church for a full service in almost a year—the urge to sing overwhelmed me. I drew on my past vocal training to control my breath and reduce the sense of being smothered by my tight N95. After wavering for a couple verses, I found my flow. My breath was moving through me. I recalled the vocal technique for a clear head tone, to picture your air issuing directly from the bridge of your nose, and imagined my rusty voice beaming straight through my mask to the altar, overcoming all barriers.

At the end of the service, the man seated in front of me turned and said, "What a treat to have such a good singer behind me. Thanks for sharing your voice." Compliment aside, the interaction itself was what touched me—the chance encounter, our physical proximity, the embodied energy of air and breath and sound waves. Having someone beyond the four walls of my house experience my presence. Sharing a fleeting moment and leaving more joyful—hopeful—for it.

Later, once I was back to the same old same old at home, I remembered the mockingbird singing at church. What might its presence have meant? I went searching for mockingbird symbology to connect the birdsong to my church experience, but I couldn't pin down any consistent interpretation of this common backyard bird. They could convey authenticity (or lack thereof), innocence, loyalty, opportunity ...all qualities that can sometimes feel in short supply in our modern era, but none that reflected the hope I felt that day while singing.

Instead, I found facts: The Northern Mockingbird, or *mimus polyglottos* ("many-tongued mimic"), can learn hundreds of songs in its lifetime, belting them out throughout the whole day and often into the night, especially during mating season. Their small gray bodies belie their outsized personalities; besides their constant singing, they fiercely protect their territories from intruders. And, most surprising to me, mockingbirds were so prized as cage birds in the nineteenth century that their numbers in the wild dropped dramatically.

This detail lit up my writerly brain. That's it! We are all caged birds, my maudlin side chirped, convinced it had pinpointed a neat metaphor for my despairing pandemic experience. But cooler heads prevailed, and I turned to art rather than science to find the meaning I was seeking.

First, I considered these lines from Maya Angelou's poem "Caged Bird":

> The caged bird sings
> with a fearful trill
> of things unknown
> but longed for still ...[2]

And then juxtaposed it with the first verse of Emily Dickinson's "'Hope' is the thing with feathers":

---

[2] https://www.poetryfoundation.org/poems/48989/caged-bird

"Hope" is the thing with feathers -
That perches in the soul -
And sings the tune without the words -
And never stops - at all - [3]

What we long for. What we hope for. Are they the same? To long for something is to yearn; it's a desire, a wish, conveying passivity. Hope, on the other hand, is active. We choose it. As Czech leader Vaclav Havel put it in *Disturbing the Peace*, "Hope is not prognostication. It is an orientation of the spirit, an orientation of the heart."

Surely few things felt more hopeless to early Christians than watching the historical Jesus suffer and die on a cross—the event we modern Christians commemorate on Good Friday. Yet there I was two thousand years later, marking the solemn occasion within a church community to remind myself that redemption is both here and on its way. Each day we experience rebirths large and small, and each day we're reminded of all that is dying. In spite of this dichotomy—or maybe because of it—we decide to hope.

The mockingbird outside the church window was oblivious to the fact that inside the church, we were mourning a sealed tomb. The blithe singer was thinking only of sunshine and fresh air and what cheery tune it would sing next. Life is far from perfect. It never will be perfect. We sing anyway.

---

[3] https://www.poetryfoundation.org/poems/42889/hope-is-the-thing-with-feathers-314

Breath Prayer for Hope

Inhale: *Fill my lungs with hope.*
Exhale: *and carry my song to the world.*

Julia Rocchi
juliarocchi.com
Amen? Questions for a God I Hope Exists

It's really a wonder that I haven't
dropped all my ideals, because they seem
so absurd and impossible to carry out.
Yet I keep them, because in spite of
everything, I still believe that people are
really good at heart.

Anne Frank

Hoping for the Best, For Real

Facing an Uncertain Future with Spiritual Resiliency

Frank Rogers Jr.

"You have a mass in your breast ducts that is producing abnormal cells. The way that it is presenting—we suspect it is cancerous ...or at least precancerous. We would like to do a surgical biopsy in which we also implant a titanium clip as a target for radiation treatments. Unfortunately, the medical equipment necessary is not available for eight weeks. It's a long wait ...but let's hope for the best."

With these words from her doctor, my wife, Alane, and I entered the winter of 2022.

As a human community, we are living through crises that can easily erode hope and engender despair—a global pandemic, gun violence in our grocery stores and elementary schools, military aggression both unprovoked and unsparing, political divides that undermine our capacities for democracy. Many of us are enduring personal crises as well—aging parents in decline without adequate healthcare resources, high school children battling mental illness, or a potential cancer diagnosis sending shivers of terror into you and your beloved. In the midst of it all, what does it mean to "hope for the best"—to find a hope that genuinely sees you through?

Hope is often misunderstood. Hope is not a wishful thinking that something we desire will happen in the future. Hope is not the naïve optimism that we will survive the pandemic unscathed, that my child will not fall prey to depression's abyss, or that my loved ones will elude cancer's invasion. The truth is that COVID-19 strikes some and not others, even with precautions in place; that mental illness afflicts innumerable teens even ones in our own family; that some masses are found malignant, and others are found benign regardless of how hard we might desire the outcome. Hope is more than mere wishing for good things to happen. It is a source of spiritual resilience.

In her book *Unstressed: How Somatic Awareness Can Transform Your Body's Stress Response and Build Emotional Resilience*, my wife, Dr. Alane Daugherty, summarizes the science around hope. Hope, she details, is a sense of confidence in one's future regardless of how bleak one's future might seem. It is an internal assurance that one can endure the circumstances of one's life with resilience and resourcefulness even when those circumstances prove to be daunting. Hope is not the fanciful thinking that the bad thing will not happen, the hope-against-hope conviction that things will go the way that we want them to even against all evidence to the contrary. Hope faces the reality of the challenges before us; and it steps toward the future that we desire with an inner strength that sustains and restores us even when the undesirable plays out before us.

This is akin to the New Testament understanding of hope. Hope is not praying to a Santa Claus God to grant us the things that we want; it is facing the future with the assurance of faith—that no matter how the future plays out, the God who has companioned us before will continue to walk with us, valleys and mountaintops alike.

How might we cultivate such resilient hope amid the challenges that we face? First, Dr. Daugherty suggests, we can draw from the strength of the past. Both as a human community and as individuals, we have faced challenges before, and we have found the resources to suffer them with resilience. We have endured the threat of scary diagnoses; we have walked with family members when the challenges they were facing seemed insurmountable; we have even faced the death of loved ones—grieving, agonizing, and finding it within us to carry on.

Second, she suggests, we can remember our way into the future. We can recall the personal resources that sustained us in the past and imagine ourselves embodying them once more in the future. The capacity for hope already dwells within us like living springs of spiritual resilience. By recollecting the felt sense of our resilience in the past, we can access those springs and visualize ourselves living into our future from the resources of our best possible self.

Finally, we can notice the springs of hope gurgling all around us. People in our communities are already facing the challenges of the day with hope. In ways both simple and extraordinary, people are rising above the drag of despair and choosing care over callousness, dignity over disrespect, a commitment to the common good over one's narrow self-interest. Medical professionals tend to the ill with kindness and self-sacrifice; a community ravaged by a school shooting grieves with one another and commits to healing together; women hold hands as they face chemotherapy together, and their husbands soothe them with ice chips and foot massages.

I noticed these springs in my wife. During the interminable eight weeks of awaiting her biopsy and treatment plan, she faced her future with hope. She did not naïvely believe that she could escape a cancer diagnosis by simply wishing it so. She confronted the very real possibility that the evidence portended cancer; and she drew on her resources to face a daunting future with resilience. She researched the breast cancer awareness three-day-walk that we would join in solidarity with other survivors; she confided in close friends and drew strength from their survivor stories; we went on weekend road trips to restore her spiritual resources; she held hands with me, sniveled with me at sappy sad songs, then flashed me the Mary Tyler Moore glance with which she could turn the world on with her smile. To be sure, she had anxious and teary nights—hope does not come without bouts with fear. Yet even fear can be faced with hope—honoring the instinctive terrors and savoring the gift of their reminder that life and love are treasures to be infinitely relished. And as she accessed the springs of resilience within her, she streamed as one with the sacred spirit that companions all in times of challenge and inspires the confidence that it all can be faced and endured.

Against the odds, the cells in Alane's breast duct were benign. With our relief was the confidence that we would have walked the other road if we had had to; as was the recognition that such is the road that many more women have to journey every day. Hoping for the best is not hoping that bad things never come our way. It is hoping that we can face both the good and the bad with a spiritual resilience that can endure all things.

It is facing the truth. And hoping for real.

Frank Rogers Jr.
cst.edu/frank-rogers-jr
Cradled in the Arms of Compassion: A Spiritual Journey from Trauma to Recovery (2023)

There is a saying in Tibetan, "Tragedy should be utilized as a source of strength." No matter what sort of difficulties, how painful experience is, if we lose our hope, that's our real disaster.

Dalai Lama XIV

Hope in All That Remains in You

Mick Silva

I believe the record will show: the times, they are still a-changin'. Thank you, Bob Dylan. But I guess if that's our only hope, I'm not comforted. When people don't believe in the dream of heaven anymore, it makes sense to claim the dream of progress instead. And maybe it's cynical, but have the times changed that much, or any of the things that really matter? I don't know.

None of us want to turn into our parents, but I wouldn't bet on being able to help it. And even if you no longer believe in a punitive, patriarchal God, you still hope for a truckload of unreasonable things. You don't quit hoping for faith just because you don't believe in theirs anymore. I don't really know how I lost mine, or when, but there are deep scars where my childhood faith used to be. I soldier on through that grief, but it'd probably be good to try and see what happened more clearly. Much as I'd like to ignore them, those marks are still there, the vestiges of my deepest hopes.

What brings this to mind, though, is my dead uncle Richard, the agnostic deadhead whose rare comments still append my old Facebook posts. He'd loved my aunt Chris intensely. Even before the call from my mom to say he'd passed, I knew it'd be his unquenchable thirst that would kill him, like Nick Cage's in *Leaving Las Vegas*. When my aunt was dying of aggressive brain cancer, he'd delivered her last request: that my younger pastor brother and I drive to Eugene, Oregon and offer a prayer. Though my only credit was being her nephew, he offered me a cigarette on his front porch. I mentioned how good it was that he was there for her, that he'd loved her well. "I have no choice," he said forcefully, then got this far-off look and repeated it. "I have no choice."

For years after, I heard it as *What else can I do but to suffer with her?* Knowing his similar melancholy disposition, that seemed logical. But I'll never forget feeling cornered and faced with the reality of his hopelessness. They say when you're cornered you either fight, flee, or freeze. I'm a freezer. My brother didn't respond either, which I was glad for, but I wished someone would say the right thing. Times always seem to change on you before you're ready. And often, you're going to feel a bit betrayed by it. You don't always get a choice. I don't think I could choose how to respond.

But the worst part was that something in me knew, even then, that this experience might crush him. And so uncertain about faith, so freshly unable as I was to claim the old religion-based magical thinking, I couldn't help or even offer some shred of hope. But I loved him for his honesty, knowing we were believers and admitting that help-lessness anyway. Let the record show as well: he had no choice. Let there be no mistake. Fight or flee, this can't be denied. We're all cornered here.

I wished I'd said it then, but he was a hero. He faced that terror alone, and when his end came, I hope that more than fear he felt that whatever-you-call-it, that "grief-hope," knowing he'd loved and been loved. We need an English word for that, like *hiraeth*, from Welsh, which is a sort of longing for an irretrievable former home. Or the German word *sehnsucht*, an irrepressible yearning for an impossible better world. But I like *saudade*, the Portuguese term for melancholic yearning, or homesickness for love lost. I hope as bereft as he was, somehow my uncle found a hint of salvation in that longing.

Maybe that's insufficient comfort. But it's all I've got. And when the big 3 a.m. feelings come, I've resolved to try and speak them in the daylight, wherever they come from. My own fear and helplessness came early on and then got reinforced when Mom and Dad didn't know how to help. But I've found if you let it, that feeling can show you how afraid people are, and more of what they carry. After all the things you've tried to dispel it—pretending, hiding, power-tripping, getting self-righteous—maybe you can accept it. Maybe it was never meant to resolve.

Can all that remains unresolved in us bring back hope? I think back to the many sermons I heard growing up and can't remember any saying something like that. But maybe if we quit rushing to nail it down with religion, the uncertainty could carve out some space for peace, if not something close to it. Maybe faith like that isn't achieved so much as received. I mean, read your Bible, but don't do it looking for certainty. I'm not sure that's in there.

As a pastor's kid I heard black and white, either/or, never both/and. Now I want to explore where I was once afraid to go and know it's okay if I never catch up. That's frustrating, but I want to include even that. I can't imagine I'll feel farther from God for that. Being free to not know feels safer somehow, like embracing surprises and interruptions, it can grow your courage to accept bigger feelings of helplessness. And God bless you, Uncle Richard. I don't know all you meant by it, but I agree—we have no choice. Letting go sucks.

The sage of Ecclesiastes said find wisdom, and maybe that just means "commit to your own becoming." I have hope that's still happening even in the 2020s. I know at least a handful of folks still daring to face the fear and trust their hearts. And that feels appropriately humble enough, to hope our old timidity is being chased off.

Maybe despite those big fears we never move past, there's hope that it could all still resolve yet.

Mick Silva
micksilva.com

Hope is not about proving anything. It's about choosing to believe this one thing, that love is bigger than any grim, bleak shit anyone can throw at us.

Anne Lamott

I'm Putting My Hope in Love

Marla Taviano

There's this show I adore called *Schitt's Creek*. It got me through a pandemic, repatriation, a breast cancer scare, and an unexpected divorce in 2020. I still watch it every night before bed to help me fall asleep.

In episode six of season three of the show, two characters are leaving their job at a motel to go to a meeting. The woman props up a "Back in 15 Minutes" sign on the front desk. The man frowns and says, "Well, it's going to take a lot longer than fifteen minutes."

To which the woman replies: "You've got to give people hope."

I feel this deep in my bones. No, I'm not talking about sticking your head in the sand or your fingers in your ears. I'm not talking about putting on a fake, happy, hopeful face in the midst of everything (marriage, country, life) going to shit all around us. And I'm *reeeeally* not talking about putting your hope in some far-off-in-the-distance possibly-a-figment-of-our-imagination afterlife.

But I still believe you've got to give people hope.

Sometimes you've got to put that sign on the desk to encourage folks (yourself included) that there's a ray of light and hope at the end of the seemingly forever-long dark tunnel. And I really do believe—despite all damning evidence to the contrary—that we have reason to keep hoping.

So, where are we supposed to find this hope? you might be asking. Good question.

It's actually in a lot of places if we can muster the energy to lift up our heads for a minute and look around. There's hope in blooming flowers. There's hope in delicious food. In your favorite hobby. In brilliant sitcoms. In the laughter of the people you love. The list is endless.

One place I've found hope lately (okay, always) is in *books*. Specifically, books written by people who have been through a whole hell of a lot and have still found something to put their hope in. Even more specifically, Black authors, Indigenous authors, and other authors of color who have found hope for centuries in this country that was built on white supremacy, stolen land, stolen bodies, stolen labor, and stolen lives—and continues to perpetuate injustice.

And, yet, they hold on to hope.

African American spirituals. Indigenous peoples saying "we're still here." People fighting to make Black Lives Matter. Queer and disabled people pushing for rights we all should have. People resisting and revolting with their actions and their words—and demonstrating love in the midst of hate.

Hope, hope, hope.

> Hope is essential to any political struggle for radical change when the overall social climate promotes disillusionment and despair.
>
> —bell hooks

> It is in collectivities that we find reservoirs of hope and optimism.
>
> —Angela Y. Davis

> We must accept finite disappointment, but never lose infinite hope.
>
> —Martin Luther King Jr.

Sometimes, when everything feels literally hopeless, I borrow the hope of others until I feel it myself. And then I pay it forward and do this for other people.

I meet a lot of folks who are at the beginning of a faith deconstruction journey, just starting to wake up, to question long-held beliefs. Their worry and fear are palpable. All they can see is the crumbling, the slippery slope, the inevitable crash, the painful burn.

They can't see a path forward. They can't see the hope. And I offer my words—and my experiences—as living breathing proof that hope is real. That there is goodness up ahead on the road, that things will not always feel as disorienting and terrifying as they do right now.

And that we can even find hope while we're in the middle of all of that.

And, unlike my regurgitated rhetoric in the books from the first few decades of my life, these days I'm not talking about the "hope of heaven." For so many people, offering platitudes about eternal happiness after you're dead is how they plan on getting through this life on earth. For others, that heaven talk is how they discourage people from speaking up against injustice in the here and now.

Enslaved people were told not to worry about their chains—they'd be free in heaven someday. People in poverty are told by colonizing missionaries that "salvation" is more important than having food to feed their starving children. Hurting people are told that God will wipe the tears from their eyes "someday." Just not today.

Back in the day, every damn thing I did had to have a "kingdom purpose," and that purpose was "saving souls." And what were they being saved from? Eternal fiery torment. What were they being saved *to*? An eternity of walking streets of gold in white robes with God.

As lovely (boring) as that sounds, I'm done with it. Now I'm like, let's just spread love and kindness and sunshine to people during their lifetime here on earth. Let's pay reparations and make things fair and give everybody access to everything they need to be whole *today*.

Let's right wrongs *right now*.

Let's live as if this one wild and precious life (shout-out to Mary Oliver) is all we have. If something fun (like mansions or gold streets or all the Thai food I can eat) comes after it, well, then that's a nice bonus.

Let's love ourselves *now*, love our neighbors *now*. Love all of everybody *now*. Love, love, love.

Where do I find hope today? I find it in *love*. The Bible has this really famous passage where it talks about these three things remaining: faith, hope, and love. "And the greatest of these is love." Paul and I butt heads a lot, but I couldn't agree with him more on this one. Love is where it's at.

I often get asked "where I've landed" regarding my faith. Nowadays, I define my faith by love. Where have I landed? I've landed on love.

And, as long as I have breath left to love, I have hope.

Marla Taviano
marlataviano.com
*jaded: a poetic reckoning with white
evangelical christian indoctrination*

Contributors

Lemuel R.T. Blackett is a writer and ordained local church pastor who has served in ministry for more than twenty years, including as a director of outreach at Guideposts. He's currently Donor and Corporate Relations Manager at Interfaith Community Services. He is the author of *Help, I'm Dealing with Trauma: Real Talk, Real Encouragement, and Real Healing*. He is a graduate of Eastern Baptist School of Religion and is pursuing an MDiv at Knox Theological Seminary. He lives in San Diego, California, with his wife Kimberlee and their three children, Brendan, Sasha, and Noah. Learn more at lemuelblackett.org.

Cynthia Vacca Davis is a semi-salty adjunct English professor with a trunk full of papers and snack wrappers. She's the author of *Intersexion: A Story of Faith, Identity, and Authenticity*. She holds an MFA in creative nonfiction, leads workshops, has written hundreds of feature stories, and has two young adult novels, *The Chrysalis* and *Drink the Rain*. When she's not home in coastal Virginia with her husband, pets, and students, she can often be found in the French Quarter of New Orleans in search of jazz and parades. Subscribe to her newsletter or follow her on social media at cynthiavaccadavis.com.

Rebekah Drumsta is the author of *When Family Hurts: 30 Days to Finding Healing and Clarity*. She has worked for various organizations including educational and mental health content development, international relations, and public speaking. She is the Chief Operating Officer of NPE Friends Fellowship, an international nonprofit which assists individuals and their families who have received unexpected results from an at-home DNA test. She is also a consultant, writer, and advocate at rebekahdrumsta.com, with the mission of supporting survivors of religious trauma. Rebekah and her family reside in Texas.

Trey Ferguson likes playing with words. Whether it be with tweets, videos, essays, sermonic presentations, Bible studies, podcasts, or speaking engagements, he's always trying to provoke an image in a seeker with some combination of words. In addition to publishing his own newsletter, The Son Do Move, and hosting the *New Living Treyslation* and *Three Black Men* podcasts, and speaking especially in churches, his forthcoming book helps our diverse world learn how to think bigger about God. Follow him at pastortrey05.com.

Brandon Darrell Lane Flanery writes about honest, messy things, specifically around faith and sexuality. He's published with the *Colorado Springs Indy* and *The Scribe*, and has academic essays with the University of Colorado at Colorado

Springs. His memoir, *Stumbling: A Sassy Memoir about Coming Out of Evangelicalism,* is about being raised in evangelical Christendom as a closeted gay man, and unwinding what is real and true for him post-closet, a journey full of trail-blazing, thorn bushes, and dead ends. He lives in Atlanta. Visit brandonflanery.com.

Matt Kendziera is a full-time speaker, podcaster, writer, and author of *Bring It Home: The Adventure of Finding Yourself after Being Lost in Religion.* He is the host of the *Chasing Goodness* podcast, engaging authors, activists, and influencers on questions that most people run from. He's also a collaborator with several other incredible organizations such as Rachel's Challenge, Ashoka, Celtic Way, and Soularize. Matt currently lives in rural Wisconsin with the love of his life, Suzie, and his two teenage children. Learn more and follow him at www.mattkendziera.com.

Kate J. Meyer, MDiv, LPC, is an ordained minister and licensed professional counselor who has worked in both private practice and hospice care. She is passionate about bringing grief into the light so that all grievers know how to move forward in a healthy, life-giving manner. Kate is the author of *Faith Doesn't Erase Grief: Embracing the Experience and Finding Hope* and *The Red Couch,* a novel about past mistakes and a challenge to overcome them. She is a dog mom living with her husband in western Michigan. Visit katejmeyer.com to join her newsletter or follow her on social media.

David Morris, PhD, is a lifelong student of psychology and religion, and the author of *Lost Faith and Wandering Souls: A Psychology of Disillusionment, Mourning, and the Return of Hope*. He has served professionally for major publishers and worked with bestselling authors and books. He is the publisher of Lake Drive Books and literary agent at Hyponymous Consulting, two innovative ventures working to specialize in authors and books that help people heal, grow, and discover. He lives with his wife in Grand Rapids, Michigan, and they have two daughters. Visit davidrmorris.me.

Scott Okamoto is a writer, musician, podcaster, and storyteller. He's spent much of his professional career teaching English at a private Christian college, and witnessing the experience of marginalized people there, which he relays in his podcast *Chapel Probation*. His book, *Asian American Apostate: Losing Religion and Finding Myself at an Evangelical University*, tells his unlikely spiritual journey, bringing together an evangelical past and an Asian American experience. He lives in Southern California with his wife and three kids. Learn more at rscottokamoto.com.

Julia Rocchi writes prose, poetry, prayers, and a lot of thank-you notes. She is the author of *Amen? Questions for a God I Hope Exists*. With an MA in writing from Johns Hopkins University, she has garnered multiple story publications and honors, including first place in the *Saturday Evening Post*'s Great American Fiction Contest. Julia also works in nonprofit marketing, facilitates gatherings, and performs improv comedy. Julia lives in Arlington, Virginia with her family. Visit juliarocchi.com to follow her blog or follow her on social media.

Frank Rogers is a professor at the Claremont School of Theology, a trained spiritual guide, a retreat leader, and the author of *Cradled in the Arms of Compassion: A Spiritual Journey from Trauma to Recovery* (2023), *Practicing Compassion, Compassion in Practice: The Way of Jesus*, and *The God of Shattered Glass*, a novel. He focuses on life-formation that is contemplative, creative, and socially liberative. He is the cofounder of the Center for Engaged Compassion (centerforengagedcompassion.com) and lives in Southern California.

Mick Silva is an author coach and writer who has worked as an acquiring editor for WaterBrook Press and Zondervan Books. He lives in Grand Rapids, Michigan, with his wife and two daughters. He cooks (badly), gardens, plays piano, and enjoys classic video games. And sometimes he writes about writing, editing, and publishing. Learn more at micksilva.com.

Marla Taviano is into books, love, justice, globes, anti-racism, blue, gray, rainbows, poems. She reads and writes for a living. She's a mom to some freaking awesome kids, wears her heart on her t-shirts, and is on a mission-quest-journey to live wholefarted (not a typo). She's the author of *unbelieve: poems on the journey to becoming a heretic* and *jaded:*

a poetic reckoning with white evangelical christian indoctrination.
Follow Marla at marlataviano.com.

About Lake Drive Books

Lake Drive Books is an independent publishing company offering books that help you heal, grow, and discover.

We offer books about values and strategies, not ideologies; authors that are spiritually rich, contextually intelligent, and focused on human flourishing; and we want to help readers feel seen.

If you like this book, or any of our other books at lakedrivebooks.com, we could use your help: please follow our authors on social media or join their email newsletters, and please especially tell others about these amazing books and their authors.

Made in United States
North Haven, CT
04 August 2023

39973295R00065